Furry Fiction is Everywhere

A Step-by-Step Guide to Writing Anthropomorphic Characters

By Ian Madison Keller

and

Mary E. Lowd

Rainbow Dog Books
Portland, OR

Cover by Ian Madison Keller

Table of Contents

Introduction

This book is for those of you who want to write furry fiction that doesn't feel like it's merely about humans in animal costumes.

Have you ever read a book or novel and wondered why they even bothered to make certain character(s) in the book something other than human? Want to avoid that in your own work?

There are some simple steps you can take to make your anthropomorphic (or furry) characters stand out on the page. This book first will go through some terminology and examples of historical furry fiction before diving into detailed how-to's, offering both help and examples.

From anthropomorphic cats to kangaroos, bats to fairies, we'll go over how to set up your species, your culture, and your world-building to set you up for success.

The tips in this book are designed to be implemented before you begin writing, while you're still working on world-building and story planning.

If you've already begun crafting your story or have a finished draft, don't worry, you can still apply the tips laid out here, but you might have a bit more work ahead of you to root out preconceived notions already set up in your world-building,

Introduction

in addition to simpler revisions to make the text itself pop with the fun details that make furry fiction so delightful.

Part 1: What is Furry?

1.1. What is Furry Fiction

What is furry?

There are almost as many answers to this question as there are people. Furry will mean something slightly different to everyone who asks. For the purpose of this book, furry is any writing that heavily features either a character with animal-like traits or an animal-like character with human-like intelligence and personality.

As you can see, this definition is rather nebulous and broad. Lots of things fall under the furry umbrella that wouldn't at first glance be considered traditionally furry.

Another term you'll encounter in this book is "scalies" which is used for non-furry creatures like lizards, dinosaurs, fish, avians and the like. Furry is generally used as the default term, with non-furred creatures lumped in under the 'furry' umbrella.

The furry fandom itself began around the 1980s, although the exact date is arguable. The 80s date gets called into question, with some arguing the fandom started even earlier, with the release of *Kimba the White Lion*, *Watership Down*, and

Disney's *Robin Hood*. Either way, furry has been around for at least forty years, and looks to be gaining in popularity with skyrocketing attendance at conventions around the world.

Although furry is primarily a visual fandom — with comics, movies, art, and costumes being the most popular aspects — there is also a large and growing literary tradition. Along with visual artists, there is a large contingent of writers, and many recurring anthologies that have been running for over a decade as of this writing. There are an increasing number of writers who can make a living writing furry fiction, either with commissioned stories or through more traditionally published works.

By picking up this book, you've expressed an interest in furry fiction, and it's a fair assumption that you are considering trying your hand at writing it, and are possibly wondering where to get started.

But before we talk about where we're going, let's first get ourselves grounded in where the genre has been.

1.2. A Historical Look

Furry in fiction has existed since humans first started writing things down, long before the furry fandom existed. Many of the oldest stories are furry stories.

There are far too many examples to list, and this book is, of course, first and foremost about writing furry, so we only intend to paint a broad overview here of some works you might want to check out for inspiration before you delve deeper into your furry writing journey.

However, if you're too eager to wait, feel free to skip ahead to Part 2 and come back to the history lesson at your leisure.

These sections are broken up between furry writings that happened before furry as a fandom existed and after.

Ancient World to 1900s

In ancient Egypt, many deities had furry characteristics or animal heads. I'm sure many of you are familiar with Anubis, god of the dead, who is often depicted as a jackal or a man with the head of a jackal.

Ancient Egypt had a lot of zoomorphism, or the tendency to view human behavior in terms of the behavior of animals. As a result, Egyptian imagery and characters tend to show up often in furry art and writing, with Anubis being one of the most popular.

In Norse paganism, the gods often consort with talking animals or shapeshift into animals. One such myth revolves around the trickster god Loki transforming into a mare and birthing the eight-legged horse Sleipnir. There is also the talking wolf Fenrir, another child of Loki, an intelligent wolf god who has many stories written about him in the Prose Edda and Poetic Edda. Similarly, Greek mythology is filled with gods, especially Zeus, transforming themselves and others into animals, not to mention figures like the centaurs and bull-headed Minotaur.

Many old religions feature animalistic gods or goddesses, or animal demi-gods.

Folklore from all over the world has many stories with animal characters, with the animal features standing in as metaphors for human strengths or weaknesses.

Reynard the fox stories originated in Europe in the late Middle Ages. The main character, Reynard, the anthropomorphic red fox, has various adventures and allegoric tales with a variety of other anthropomorphic animals that satirize religion and parody other popular tales from the times.

Ancient Japanese folklore has the kitsune, a magical talking fox that can transform into a human; kappa, an amphibious human-like creature with webbed feet and a turtle shell on their back; and the tanuki, a Japanese racoon dog that can transform into anything and frequently likes to mess with

5

humans. There are also many tales of interspecies marriage, one of the most famous being the tale of the crane wife, about a crane woman who marries a human man.

The epic poem Beowulf, written between 700 and 1000 AD, starts with the titular character, Beowulf, a young warrior, fighting against Grendel, an anthropomorphic creature terrorizing a village. His killing of Grendel angers Grendel's mother, who swears revenge and hunts and attacks Beowulf. The poem ends with Beowulf slaying a dragon, but he is mortally wounded and also dies.

And of course, Aesop's Fables are filled with animal characters.

The Rise of Science Fiction as a Genre

As science fiction became its own genre, a number of books with furry creatures came onto the scene. There are far too many to list them all, but below is a selection of titles that often pop up in best-of lists or recommendations.

1894 *The Jungle Book* by Rudyard Kipling, a boy being raised in the jungle by a variety of talking animals

1903 *The Call of the Wild* by Jack London, a dog is stolen from California and sold as a sled-dog during the 1890s Klondike Gold Rush in Alaska.

1902 *The Tale of Peter Rabbit* by Beatrix Potter, along with her other works, this illustrated story depicts a world of animals living at our feet but dressing and acting much like us.

1908 *The Wind in the Willows* by Kenneth Grahame, four anthropomorphized animals — mole, rat, toad, and badger — living in a pastoral English countryside.

1923 *Bambi: A Life in the Woods* by Felix Salten, coming-of-age story that follows a young roe deer as he grows up.

1945 *Animal Farm* by George Orwell, a group of farm animals overthrow the humans on their farm and take it over for themselves.

1950-1954 *Kimba the White Lion* by Osamu Tezuka, Japanese serialized graphic novel about a talking, young, white lion.

1951 *The Day of the Triffids* by John Wyndham, an aggressive species of carnivorous plants called triffids start killing people.

1959 *The Rescuers* by Margery Sharp, the first in The Rescuers series, a mouse led Prisoners' Aid Society rescues humans from captivity. Disney based the movie *The Rescuers* on some of the novels in this series.

1962 *Little Fuzzy* by H. Beam Piper, a novel about humans determining whether a small fuzzy species discovered on a colony planet is sapient. Nominated for a Hugo.

1965 *Watership Down* by Richard Adams, anthropomorphized rabbits trying to set up a new home after the destruction of their burrow.

1968 *Dragonflight* by Anne McCaffrey, the first in the Dragonriders of Pern series, a young woman establishes a telepathic bond with a dragon. The novellas that make up this work won a Hugo and a Nebula Award.

1968 *The Last Unicorn* by Peter S. Beagle, a unicorn who believes she is the last of her kind travels to discover what happened to the others.

1973 *The Cat Who Wished to be a Man* by Lloyd Alexander, a cat gets his wish to become human and learns to regret his choice.

1977 *Midnight at the Well of Souls* by Jack L. Chalker, the first book in The Saga of the Well World series, a team of human astronauts stumble onto a high-tech world that transforms them into a variety of anthropomorphic animals.

Modern-Day - 1980s to Present (2021)

Like the previous section, this list is in no way exhaustive! This is a selection of some of the most popularly recommended furry fiction books.

1981 *Scruffy* by Jack Stoneley, about a stray dog trying to survive on the streets of a big city and rescue her pack from the pound.

1981 *The Pride of Chanur* by C. J. Cherryh, the first in the Chanur series. Nominated for a Hugo and Locus Award. A lion-like alien and her crew pick up a mysterious human, lost on a space station of other aliens, and have to protect him and figure out what to do with him.

1983 *Spellsinger* by Alan Dean Foster, the first in the Spellsinger series. A human man is transported into a world of sentient animals, and helps a tortoise wizard perform magic with rock music. *Content warning on this one for heavy objectification of women and implied rape.

1983 *Startide Rising* by David Brin, part of The Uplift Saga. Dolphin and human crew members battle to survive after crashing on a water world. In The Uplift Saga, no species has reached sentience without a patron race, but who uplifted humankind?

1986 *Redwall* by Brian Jacques, the first book in the Redwall series. Adventures of anthropomorphic woodland animals living in Redwall Abbey and the surrounding woods.

1986 *The Architect of Sleep* by Steve Boyett, a human man stumbles into a different universe where the dominant species are anthro raccoons with wild west-era technology.

1987 *The Crown Jewels* by Walter John Williams, first in the Majistral series, about a minor human aristocrat and an allowed burglar in a galactic empire that has long since conquered and assimilated humanity, where humans are a minority.

1993 *Forests of the Night* by S. Andrew Swann, a genetically altered tiger investigates a murder in future Cleveland.

1999 *The Thirteen and a Half Lives of Captain Bluebear* by Walter Moers, a human-sized bear with blue fur retells adventures of his many different lives.

2003 *Song of the Beast* by Carol Berg, a disgraced bard with broken hands finds magic and solace with an enemy dragon.

2004 "St. Ailbe's Hall" by Naomi Kritzer, a short story published in Strange Horizons magazine. An enhanced Siberian husky wants to attend church, but the human congregation is not happy about it.

2005 *Furry! Best in Show collection* edited by Fred Patten, an anthology collecting the best-loved furry short stories previously published from 1990 to 2005. Won an Ursa Major Award.

2008 *Dragon's Wild* by Robert Lynn Asprin, an urban fantasy about a con-artist that discovers he is a dragon.

2008 *Waterways* by Kyell Gold, a coming-of-age story about a young gay otter finding love with a black fox.

2011 *Fuzzy Nation* by John Scalzi, a modern-day retelling/fanfiction of H. Beam Piper's classic *Little Fuzzy*, published with permission of Piper's estate.

2012 *The Ursa Major Award Anthology,* edited by Fred Patten, a collection of Ursa Major Award-winning short stories previously published from 2001 to 2011.

2004 - 2019 *HEAT* from Sofawolf Press, an annual all-orientations erotic anthology featuring a mixture of short stories, comics, poetry, and art. The final issue was published in 2019 at Midwest FurFest.

2005 - Present *FANG* from Bad Dog Books, an annual gay erotica anthology of furry short stories and novellas.

2007 - Present *ROAR* from Bad Dog Books, a spin-off of *FANG*, this is an annual general audience anthology of furry short stories and novellas.

2015 *Barsk: The Elephant's Graveyard* by Lawrence M. Schoen, in the far future, uplifted anthropomorphic elephants fight to save their rainy world of Barsk. Cóyotl Award winner.

2019 *The Cóyotl Awards Anthology* edited by Fred Patten, collects the best winners and nominees from the first eight years of the Cóyotl Awards to showcase a sample of the best authors the furry community has to offer.

Many, many more books have been released within the furry fandom during the last few years, but it's hard to know yet, without the perspective of passing time, which ones will stand out as historically important.

1.3 Furry Literature and Writing Now

Ursa Major Awards, or U.M.A.

More formally known as the Annual Anthropomorphic Literature and Arts Award, the Ursa Major Awards are presented annually for excellence in furry arts. They're intended to be furry's equivalent to the Hugo Award. Votes are made by the public and compiled by a committee.

Started in 2001, there are several categories for furry writing including Best Novel, Best Short Fiction, Best Other Literary Work, Best Non-Fiction Work, Best Graphic Story, Best Comic Strip, and Best Magazine.
This is the longest running and most famous of the furry writing awards. In addition to listing all the nominees and winners of the Ursa Major Awards on their website, they also keep a list of Recommended Anthropomorphic Works from each year, submitted by the public. It is a great resource to find furry writing.

https://ursamajorawards.org/

The Furry Writers' Guild, or FWG

Founded in 2011, the Furry Writers' Guild's mission is to promote the writing of anthropomorphic fiction in all genres and categories.

As of the writing of this book, anyone who has had one work of fiction with an anthropomorphic character published in a paying market or two works published in non-paying markets qualifies for membership. Membership in the guild is free.

The guild has a Telegram, Discord, and forum where furry writers can interact, talk about writing and publishing, and find out about open calls for furry centered stories. It's a warm and welcoming community where many writers have found support and camaraderie.

The guild has a monthly blog that interviews furry writers. The website has a list of all members as well as a list of recommended reading for various categories along with NSFW warnings.

In 2020, the Guild put on the online convention "Oxfurred Comma" and released a flash fiction collection of the same name. They also released *Tales from the Guild: World Tour* in 2018 and *Tales from the Guild: Music to Your Ears* in 2014.

https://furrywritersguild.com/

The Cóyotl Awards

Founded in 2012 as a way for the Furry Writers' Guild to recognize excellence in anthropomorphic literature. Works are nominated and voted on by members of the Guild, although nominated works do not have to be written by members.

The Cóyotl Awards have categories for Best Novel, Best Novella, Best Short Story, and Best Anthology. The award is a plush coyote and certificate.

https://coyotlawards.com

Regional Anthropomorphic Writers Retreat (RAWR)

A five-day writing retreat led by Kyell Gold and Ryan Campbell. Started in 2016, the retreat takes place in California.

RAWR is patterned after Clarion, the science fiction and fantasy writing retreat, which both Gold and Campbell have attended.

RAWR is focused on helping writers of anthropomorphic fiction enhance their professional networks, confidence, and writing skills by utilizing a structured and intense experience. Focused instruction, one-on-one coaching, constructive criticism, socialization opportunities, and post-event communication.

http://www.rawr.community/

Leo Literary Awards

Started in 2017 by the Furry Book Review, the goal of the Leo Literary Awards is to highlight exceptional works of literature in the furry fandom.

Works are nominated by the writers and editors in the furry fandom. Voting is done by a panel of 5 to 10 judges made up of both furry and non-furry writers. The panel of judges changes from year to year.

The Leo Literary Awards have categories for Novels, Novellas, Short Stories, Anthologies, Poems, Nonfiction, and Book Covers. Unlike other awards, there is not one clear winner or best work. All works that pass a benchmark score by the judges are awarded plush lions and certificates.

https://furrybookreview.wixsite.com/blog/leo-awards

Part 2: Types and Species

2.1. Type Versus Species

The first question when it comes to furry fiction is, what kind of animal are you dealing with?

There are two dimensions to this question: type and species. Type refers to the way your furry species presents their intelligence, whereas species is the base animal used to build the furry race you're writing about.

2.2. Types

Type Introduction

Before you get into actually writing furry fiction, you need to figure out what type of furry characters you'll be dealing with. There are a lot of standard tropes for different types of furry characters that have already been established by the oeuvre of furry fiction. While it's great to come up with your own, original, ideas, there's no need to reinvent the wheel when it comes to the basic backstory for why animal characters exist.

Or if you do want to invent an entirely new kind of wheel, it helps to know what's already out there.

Now if you've read a lot of the books listed in the previous section or perhaps other, more recent furry books, you might already be familiar with many of these concepts. But for those who aren't, this section will give an overview of the different origin stories you can give your furry species and what sets each apart.

Aliens

One popular choice for explaining animal characters: *Space! The Final Frontier.* One easy origin story that doesn't tie you to using real-life animal analogues is to make your furry species originate somewhere other than Earth.

Want to make a cat/octopus hybrid species that has fur, big soulful eyes, and suckered tentacles? Aliens!

Keep in mind, though, the more alien you make the species, the harder you'll have to work to have your readers picture and empathize with your characters. A story from the point of view of a very alien species is one of the hardest to write.

Very often stories with furry aliens also feature humans, usually as the point of view character. Either aliens come to earth and meet humans or humans meet aliens while flying around in the stars. In alien/human furry stories, some of the conflict naturally arises from how the humans interact with the (often newly discovered) aliens. These are great settings for fish out of water tales (maybe literally?) or stories of war. Though it can also be wonderful to depict a far future setting with humans and furry aliens coexisting peacefully and find the conflict in the story elsewhere.

Humans are not a requirement in these kinds of stories. Maybe your story takes place on a distant planet, or planets, between several different alien species without a human in sight.

Of course, one of the downsides of the alien origin story is you'll have to do more world-building than you might have to do with an earth-based story setting.

We'll go into this more in later sections, but think about where your story takes place when you have alien furry species. An alien origin story fits best with science fiction or near contemporary setting. Although this does not preclude you from plopping aliens into an epic fantasy tale, but the writing will have to be handled carefully, guiding the reader into believing in the unusual combination of tropes, or else risk breaking a lot of the reader's expectations, and possibly putting them off your book, or causing them to stop reading entirely. Blended genres can have a magical quality when they work, but if done poorly, they'll just be confusing.

A few examples of furry alien species in popular media would be the Wookies and Ewoks in Star Wars; the lion-like Hani in C. J. Cherryh's *Chanur* series; or the range of alien races that humans discover in David Brin's *Uplift* series.

Things to keep in mind when preparing to write furry aliens:

- Are there humans in your story? If so, how do they get along with the alien species?
- Are there multiple alien species? Are they from the same planet or multiple planets?
- Atmosphere - what do your aliens breathe? If there are humans in the story or other alien species, they might require different atmospheres or living conditions.
- Setting - does the story take place on Earth, in space, on some other planet or planets?

Answering these questions will get you well on the way to developing solid world-building for your story.

Uplifted Animals

Uplifted animals are ones that were changed, either by humans or by some other means, to have human-like levels of intelligence, and usually, but not always, to be anthropomorphic. The uplifting can come through magical or scientific means.

An example of this type in recent furry literature would be the Fant race of uplifted anthropomorphic elephants from Lawrence M. Shoen's *Barsk* novel series; cats, dogs, and otters (and later squirrels and octopuses) in Mary's *Otters in Space* series; or the rats in *Mrs. Frisby and the Rats of NIMH* by Robert C. O'Brien.

The method of uplifting can and will vary. Humans are sometimes still around, like in Mrs. Frisby, or they can be long gone with only the uplifted animals remaining, like in *Barsk* or *Otters in Space*.

Sometimes the uplifted animals know how and why they were uplifted, but it's also possible they don't know the particulars and must struggle to understand their place in the universe.

When deciding to write about uplifted animals, here are some questions you'll need to consider as you start your world-building:

- How long ago did the uplifting happen?
- If it happened recently some conflicts you might be writing about are the animals coming to grips with their newly-found intelligence or about how the uplifting affects the world at large.
- If the uplifting happened far in the past, how has that affected history?
- Do the animals know how they were uplifted and why?
  - Perhaps they know the answer to one question, but not both. Maybe this is a bone of contention between

different factions or philosophers. Religion might be based around the time of uplifting.

- If it was humans that did the uplifting, are they still around?
  - If they are, are humans considered a lower class? Higher? For what purpose were animals uplifted? If it was companionship, the animals might be treated like pets or children. Or if the purpose was to change them to perform some task humans can't or didn't want to do themselves, the uplifted ones might be enslaved or forced into a lower class, seen as 'less than.' It's important when writing about a situation like this to keep in mind how your world-building might be construed allegorically. We'll discuss this more later in the book.
- If humans are no longer around, are they worshiped as gods? Maligned as villains? Or maybe the uplifted animals don't give the missing humans much thought or don't know much about them. If they don't know much about them, do they crave this missing information? Or have they perhaps replaced it with different, possibly even conflicting mythologies?
- If some other method caused your uplifting, perhaps an accidental or environmental factor, think about how and why it came about and how that might affect your world and story.
- Has the factor been stopped? Or is it an ongoing situation?
- Were all individuals uplifted suddenly at the same time? Or did it happen more slowly, possibly at different rates for different individuals? Are there still feral/non-uplifted versions of the uplifted species?
- Are members of the society trying to stop, encourage, or even reverse the process of uplift? Quite likely, there would be differing factions with different goals, possibly leading to interesting political conflicts.

Gene-modded Humans

Most often found in sci-fi or near future stories, gene-modded human furry characters are humans who have used some kind of technology to give themselves animal features or become animal hybrids. This can be as small as giving themselves heightened senses to as large as full-body modifications that change the human's form entirely to animal, or anything in between.

Watts Martin's *Kismet's* main character, a human-rat hybrid, would be a good example of this type of furry character, as would the rabbits in Phil Guesz's *The First Book of Lapinism*.

This is very common in sci-fi, to the point it is considered a trope, but it could work in a magical setting too, with magic replacing technology's role in creating the hybrids.

Things to consider with gene-modded humans:

- Are full humans still around? If so, how do they feel about the modified people?
- What are the ethics surrounding gene-modding children? Is there a standard age of consent for getting gene-modded?
- Is there a hierarchy to those who have gotten the modifications? For example, predator vs prey species?
- Are the modifications easy to come by? Expensive? Reversible? Popular and desirable or rare and weird?
- Is it common to mix and match species or to stick with just one? Why? Do communities spring up surrounding particular choices of mod?

As you can see, all of these science fiction options for explaining furry characters immediately lead to fascinating questions that help flesh out the world those characters will live in and, in many cases, suggest potential sources of conflict and plotlines.

Talking Animals

Commonly referred to as Secret Life of Animals, talking animal stories feature furry species who are usually feral in the sense that their bodies are shaped like normal animals, but they have human levels of intelligence. Usually, though not always, they can talk in some fashion, even if only to each other.

While it's common for the furry characters in Secret Life of Animal stories to be unable to speak to the humans around them, sometimes one of the story twists is that one specific human or perhaps a class of humans (such as trained mages or those with a specific mutation) can communicate with the furry characters.

A popular setting for talking animal stories is in human households, where the pets go on adventures that they try to keep secret from their bumbling, oblivious owners.

Another frequent setting for these types of stories is in the woods, where forest creatures often need to fight back against the encroaching humans.

Call of the Wild by Jack London would be a good example of this type of book, one where the humans cannot understand the animals, but the animals show above-average intelligence and drive.

The Warriors cat clan books by Erin Hunter would be another more recent example, with warring cat clans living in secret in the human world.

The other place you'll frequently see talking animals is in a mascot position, such as a witch's cat or mage's familiar, with the rest of the cast being human, anthro, or some combination thereof.

Things to consider when using talking animals:

- Who can hear and understand the talking animal characters?
- How intelligent are your animals?
  - This might vary considerably from character to character, of course, but think about the average or baseline intelligence of your animals - is it equivalent to the adult humans around them? Or more like young children?
- Do they have any way to use tools? This can be hand-waved quite a bit (even if they don't have actual hands) with the use of mouths, tails, and fumbling with paws.
- If your story has humans, how much are they aware of the antics of your talking animals? Are they background obstacles to be worked around or active in the plot and interacting with your animals?

It is also possible to write stories about the secret lives of animals where the animals never literally talk or do anything that a normal animal in the real world couldn't do. For instance, Garth Stein's *The Art of Racing in the Rain* is about a dog who never does anything that a dog couldn't do, but we get to listen to the dog's thoughts throughout his life, learning about his owner's travails.

Another example is Robert Bakker's *Raptor Red* which theorizes about what life might have been like in the prehistoric past for a pair of velociraptor sisters. His book stays as close to realistic as possible, while giving the reader a glimpse into the main raptor's thoughts and feelings. Stories like this come with a lot of constraints, but they can also be very rewarding.

Mythicals and Fairytales

Mythicals is a large category, encompassing dragons, gods, creatures of legend, centaurs, shapeshifters, werewolves, selkies, taurs (from centaurs to sphinxes), and more. Mythical furry characters show up most often in fantasy or urban fantasy and usually feature magic or magical-like abilities.

This pool is deep so we're only going to skim the surface here.

Many books that feature mythicals have a whole cast of different furry species. Often in fantasy you'll have dragons, kobolds, goblins, fairies, werewolves, and more. Be critical about what you need to tell your story. It is possible to go overboard on introducing new species to the reader. We're not counting background species here. If you mention mermaids, you don't need to necessarily show them to the reader right away.

When deciding to use mythicals, often a place to start is the myths and legends around the species you have picked. As with everything in writing feel free to ignore or throw out what you don't like.

This format is especially popular in epic and urban fantasy. One example of an urban fantasy would be the *Dragon's Wild* series by Robert Lynn Aspirin, with mythical dragons living in the contemporary world in secret.

All of Terry Pratchett's *Discworld* series is an example of an epic fantasy with various races and mythical creatures populating its pages, and Seanan McGuire's *October Daye* series features a variety of beings in the fairy realm, including cat shape shifters and selkies.

Some of the most common mythicals to regularly pop up in furry fiction are dragons, gryphons, and taurs.

A taur is a character with a human-like or anthro upper body and a feral lower body with four legs, effectively giving any taur character six limbs. Centaurs are the most common example, but any animal can be made into a taur with any combination of upper and lower halves.

Gryphons are a very popular type of mythical to appear in furry fiction. Jess E. Owen's series, *The Summer King Chronicles*, is entirely centered on gryphons. While the classic gryphon is a combination of an eagle's head and wings on a lion's body (possibly with an eagle's talons for the front feet), it's also possible to create gryphons by combining any bird with any feline - such as the snow leopard/snowy owl gryphon in Mary's story "Frankenstein's Gryphon." You can even stretch the definition further, replacing the cat half with other options. Though, if you choose a hoofed animal to replace the feline half, then your gryphons will begin to blur into hippogriffs.

Finally, we can't leave this section before mentioning dragons. Classical western dragons are scaly with bat-like wings and eastern dragons are long and furry noodles with no wings. Wyverns are usually a dragon with wings for arms. Dragons are depicted with a large variety of sizes and magical powers. Sometimes in urban fantasies they are even shapeshifters, taking the form of humans at times, like in Robert Lynn Asprin's *Dragon's Wild*.

Some things to consider when using mythical creatures in your writing:

- Does your world have magic and can your mythicals use magic?
- What are the rules around the different mythicals' powers?
- Are there humans in your story?
- How do your mythicals get along with the other intelligent creatures in the world? Are they hidden from the normal world or readily incorporated into it?

Fox in Starbucks

In this style, animals have basically replaced people in the world, with no real explanation. The characters' animal traits are not very strong, and the animals are just there for flavor or metaphors.

Often there's not much world-building around why people are all animals, and the world they populate simply reflects our own, real world. Instead of explaining how and why animal people exist, they just are.

A couple of examples of this style would be *Queen of Arts* by Frances Pauli, *Smiley and the Hero* by Ryan Campbell, or the video game *Night in the Woods*.

In *Queen of Arts*, the main character is a bear who likes knitting and is best friends with a rabbit. The world is basically modern-day, but with animals.

Smiley and the Hero is the fantasy version of Fox in Starbucks, with animals replacing humans but in a more rustic, fantasy world.

And in *Night in the Woods*, the setting is a contemporary small town populated with various animal people, including a cat, a gator, a fox, and a bear.

This style is most common in contemporary settings, but like any of these categories it can be mixed with any genre, as shown by *Smiley and the Hero*'s fantasy fairytale setting and *Night and the Woods'* contemporary horror pastiche.

Some things to consider with the Fox in Starbucks style:

- Do your animal people have tails? Does their animal physiology affect their furniture or buildings at all? It doesn't have to, but it can provide interesting details when it does.
- What's the mix between human intelligence and animal instincts/ characteristics? For example, can your birds still fly and your dogs track by scent? Do predator animals still feel a drive to hunt prey animals, such as in

Paru Itagaki's *Beastars*? Or have they outgrown that drive such as in *Zootopia*?

- Just generally, what kind of changes have been made in the world to accommodate these animal people, if any?

Anything Goes

As distinct from Fox in Starbucks, this style of anthropomorphic character exists in a world where humans are still around. The most famous examples of this would be the TV show *Bojack Horseman* or the point reached at the end of George Orwell's *Animal Farm* when the pigs, who have taken over, attain the full level of interacting like the humans in the rest of the world. In a sense, *Animal Farm* starts as Secret Life of Animals and then transcends to the Anything Goes style.

Anything Goes is the grab-bag of anthropomorphic animals, and it's probably more common in visual art forms at this time. However, as audiences keep getting more familiar and comfortable with furry styles of story-telling, they're more and more open to out-there aesthetics like those seen in *BoJack Horseman*. When *BoJack Horseman* started in 2014, it was a very unusual and edgy show. After six seasons, it was Netflix's most popular and long-running series, spawning the sort-of spin-off *Tuca & Bertie*. What was strange and confusing has become an accepted and beloved style of story-telling. This is the arc of furry fiction, and it's been happening with the genre overall as well.

Things to consider when writing an Anything Goes style story:

- Figure out the rules of your universe and be consistent. Or if you choose to eschew consistency, make sure aesthetics of your piece are compelling enough to draw the reader along through the inconsistencies.

- Are your furry characters a metaphor for something like in *Animal Farm*? If so, keep that in mind while writing to make sure that metaphor comes through to the reader. And even if you don't intend for your characters to be taken as allegorical, you should probably watch out for unintended ways that readers may see them as allegorical anyway.

2.3. Species

We'll talk about how to pick what species to pick for your specific characters later in the section on characters, but for now, it's good to think about what kind of animals even exist in the world that you're building. So, let's do a rundown of the different options.

Mammals

Mammals are a huge category, ranging from foxes to whales to bats. Domestic to wild animals. Horses to monkeys. Wolves to red pandas. Mammals dwell on the land, in the water, and even in the air. There is a huge variety and diversity to pick from.

Since there are so many kinds of mammals, and both writers and readers themselves fall into that category, mammal species are by far the most popular and common in anthropomorphic fiction, especially land-dwelling ones. They're familiar, comfortable, and easy for humans to relate to.

The examples of mammalian furry characters in arts and literature are far too numerous to list, and the diversity of specific species is far too wide for us to list them all here. However, we'll discuss a lot of factors to consider when writing about mammalian species in the next section.

Lizards and Amphibians

Otherwise known as "scalies"; keep in mind their cold-bloodedness. Alligators to geckos, snakes, frogs, and chameleons.

A few examples would be Kaa the python from Kipling's *The Jungle Book*, Chet Gecko from Bruce Hale's *The Chameleon Wore Chartreuse,* or the snakes in Frances Pauli's *Serpentia* series.

Things to consider with lizards or amphibian species:

- Are your scaled creatures cold-blooded and subjected to the disadvantages inherent in that? Especially relevant in a world with warm-blooded counterparts.
- For amphibians, do they dry out and die when away from water for too long?
- Do they shed their skins in order to grow?
- If they are snakes, do they have hands? It can be okay in furry fiction to alter the basic anatomy of the species' base animal. However, there are other options, such as snakes using their tails, telekinetic abilities, or even mechanical cyborg arms.

Birds

Feathers and beaks can provide a lot of world-building opportunities. Birds can range from eagles to chickens, penguins to cassowaries.

A few examples are the owls from Kathryn Lasky's *Guardians of Ga'Hoole* series or the canary from E.B. White's *Stuart Little*.

Things to consider with bird species:

- Can your birds fly/swim etc. in the same way as their base species?
- Do they have hands? Perhaps their wings are hand-like? If not, how do they manipulate things or tools?
- Do they still lay eggs?

Water-dwelling Creatures

This is a huge area, encompassing fish, sharks, marine invertebrates like jellyfish or octopuses, water-dwelling mammals like dolphins and whales, and more.

Some examples of this in popular fiction would be Mira Grant's *Into the Drowning Deep* with her intelligent deep sea creatures or Nnedi Okorafor's *Lagoon* with underwater aliens attempting to make contact with humans. Those are both from the point of view of humans.

In a slightly different take, Lynnea Glasser's *The Sea Eternal* is a choose-your-own-adventure text game that takes place entirely underwater with whales and mermaids.

Then of course, there are the dolphins in David Brin's *Startide Rising* and also the popular video game *Ecco the Dolphin*.

Things to consider with water-dwelling species:

- Can your intelligent water creatures leave the water?
- Do they have legs/arms or are they stuck in a wheelchair or pulling themselves about awkwardly when on land?
- Do they suffer if they are away from water too long?
- Can they breathe without water?
- How do they communicate?

Plants

Plant-based furry species are rarely seen but can be a lot of fun. We're including them because both of us are partial to them, having made use of several plant-based species across our various books.

A plant-based species makes the most sense in a science fiction setting as an alien species or in fantasy as a magical race. But don't let that stop you from using plants as another type! The TV show *Tuca & Bertie* makes use of some fascinating anthro plant characters who seem quite surreal to begin with, but then simply become part of the world.

Probably the most famous examples of intelligent plants would be the Ents from *The Lord of the Rings* by JRR Tolkien, Groot from Guardians of the Galaxy, the plant men of Barsoom from Edgar Rice Burroughs' Martian novels, and the carnivorous triffids from *Day of the Triffids* by John Wyndham.

Things to consider with plant-based species:

- How do they get nutrients? Are they photosynthetic or have they evolved to eat with a mouth?
- Does reproduction still happen from seeds?
- Locomotion - are they tied to the land and able to move (or move slowly like the Ents) or can they travel freely? Perhaps this can change at different points in the species' lifespan.
- What words do they use for the different stages of their lives, from young to old?

In both Mary and Ian's novels that feature plant species, the children are planted in a garden as seeds. They grow, unable to move, until they are old enough to pull up their roots. At that point the roots become legs, and they are fully ambulatory as adults.

However, that is where the similarities end. Ian's Kin species look more like elves whereas Mary's Doraspians look like bushes, using flowers to mimic mammalian traits like ears and eyes.

Bugs

After plants, bugs are probably the least seen anthro species. There are so many types of bugs that we'll only broadly brush over this category. From butterflies to beetles, there is a massive variety of creatures to pick from.

Most commonly, bug characters are written as feral rather than anthro. Often, they're simply used as frightening villains or bogeymen. From venom, to fangs, stingers, and more, insects or bugs have a variety of deadly protections.

A few great examples of bug characters in fiction would be the bees in Laline Paull's *The Bees,* Charlotte the spider from E.B. White's *Charlotte's Web*, or Miss Spider from Roald Dahl's *James and the Giant Peach.*

Things to consider when writing bug characters:

- What characteristics do they maintain if they have anthro forms?
- What size are they?
- Do they have a hive-based societal structure?
- Do they undergo a chrysalis or cocoon phase, radically changing the shape of their body from one point in their life-cycle to another?

Dinosaurs and Other Prehistoric Creatures

One really fun type of animal to write about is dinosaurs. Whenever working with dinosaur or other prehistoric creatures as characters, a few questions immediately pop up — how did they survive until now? Were they brought back into the world by scientists? If so, why? Or were they hiding somewhere, out of sight from the rest of the world? If so, where? Or possibly, are you writing a story set a long time ago, such as Robert Bakker's *Raptor Red*?

Answering these questions will give you a head start on world-building and possibly even determining your story's plot. Also, dinosaurs are simply a lot of fun, whether you're working with old-style dinos that look more like lizards or ones based on the more scientifically up-to-date understanding that they looked more like birds.

Although dinosaurs show up in a lot of novels, they are not often intelligent. A few examples of intelligent dinos in fiction would be Robert J. Sawyer's *Quintaglio Ascension Trilogy* that features an evolved T-Rex and sentient dinos, or Barry B. Longyear's *The Homecoming* science fiction novel with "long-absent reptiles" in spaceships returning to earth. They also appear in Mary's *Otters in Space* series, again, returning to earth in spaceships after a long absence.

Part 3: Building your Furry Race

3.1. Anthro vs. Feral

Now that you've decided on Type and Species (possibly even a variety of species to fill out your world), you have one more decision to make before you can build your furry race.

Are they going to be anthropomorphic or feral?

This question might have already been decided on by your type, as, for example, talking animals are (almost) always feral. However, if not, you'll need to decide now.

Anthro vs. Feral - What's the Difference?

Anthropomorphic, otherwise known as anthro, characters generally have a more standard human-like shape, walking on two legs and using hands to manipulate objects.

Feral characters are sometimes referred to as 'talking animals' or animals that generally retain their natural shape but have the ability of speech and human levels of intelligence. Feral races usually have a more animal-like form without hands and walk on whatever number of legs the species usually has.

A feral dolphin or fish would have none, but a feral octopus would probably have eight tentacles rather than legs.

This is the first decision you'll need to make before jumping farther into your world-building and characters: what kind of furry creatures populate the pages of your story?

This is not a "pick one" question. Feel free to mix and match! Perhaps your werewolves share the pages of your novel with talking animals, or aliens live alongside gene-modded humans.

An example of this would be a world with dragon riders, where both the dragon and the rider are furry. The dragon would be feral and the rider anthro.

A real-world book example is Mary's *Entanglement Bound* - the living spaceship, a space whale, is feral, while many of her crew are anthro.

For those who can't decide: why not both? It's perfectly valid to have an anthro species that also has a feral form it can shift into. Or maybe they can drop down to all fours and run around that way. For instance, the cait sidhe in Seanan McGuire's *October Daye* series can shift between a humanoid form, retaining a few aesthetic traits of their cat-nature, such as tabby-striped hair and unusual eyes, and a fully feline form.

Whereas in Ian's *Flower's Fang* series, the wolf creatures switch between using two or four legs as needed without their actual bodies changing. It's fantasy already, so don't worry too much about bending the rules of how real life works or getting too bogged down in specific details of the transition. Just be sure to be upfront with readers as to whether your characters are turning into an entirely new form, or just standing up.

Go through the following checklists to set up each race in your world. You'll need to make these decisions for each anthro or feral race that you want to populate the world of your novel or comic. If they're shifters, with an anthro and feral form, you'll need to do both checklists. One for each form.

Of course, if you have hundreds of possible species that might show up in your story in a mythical or *Zootopia*-like world, that doesn't mean you need to build out each and every one of them. Determine which ones show up as active characters and only spend the time to make what you need. Just keep other species that you didn't build up in the back of your mind as you complete the rest of your world-building. If you add a new species later, come back and complete this checklist for that new race.

If you aren't sure what species you want to make your characters yet, skip ahead to Part 5: Characters, where we'll go more into how to determine the species of your major and minor characters. Then once you have a list of which species you'll be writing about, you can come back to this chapter.

A link to download a condensed PDF version of these checklists for feral and anthro species can be found in the resource section at the end.

3.2. Furry Species Checklist - Anthro

Each anthropomorphic species will have different characteristics that set it apart from the other species in your world. You can start with a base species (like a tortoise) and go down through the checklist, thinking how you'd like the anthro version to work in your world, or you can make-up your own species, using this list of questions to consider as you build.

Hands

Anthro characters walk on two legs and have hands or paws they can use to manipulate things like a human would.

Whatever word you use to refer to your species' hands is a matter of style and personal preference. We'll go over this more in Part 6: Writing, but whichever you use, be sure to be consistent, or at least pay close attention to the aesthetics and clarity of a scene when switching between different words so as not to confuse your reader.

You can also use different words to refer to the hands of different species. For example, a lizard species might use 'hand' while a cat species might use 'paw' or 'hand-paw.' However, be aware that using 'paws' to refer to hands might cause some confusion when you need to distinguish between hands and feet, since paws could potentially refer to either.

Hooves

What about species that don't have direct hand analogs, such as ungulates like horses, deer, rhino, cattle, etc?

With hooved species, there are a few options for hands. You could have your 'hooves' be described as 'hands,' 'hooves,' 'hoof-hands', or the like. With writing, you can get away with not describing how hooves are working as hands, but be sure you know how your world works. If it becomes important later you won't be fumbling to figure it out.

A few options are keratin-tipped fingers, normal hands with thicker than normal fingernails, split hooves that can grip like crab-pincers, or regular hooves that the characters somehow (perhaps clumsily) use to manipulate things.

If you use either of the last two options, be sure to note that hooved characters might struggle with using objects designed for hands or paws. Adding details like that kind of struggle into your writing will give your world depth.

Of course, these are just suggestions. Use your imagination.

Wings

If your species has wings, and you are anthropomorphizing it, you have a few options.

The first is giving your species arms *and* wings. Yes, this does give your species six limbs. Who cares, it's fiction! However, it does make you need to think more about the world-building, like how to sit in chairs, clothing design, and more. We'll get into that more in Part 4: World-building, but it's something to be aware of.

The second option is making the species' wings serve as arms and giving them some kind of hand at the end to manipulate things. For example, the birds in *Bojack Horseman* work this way, and they can still fly.

It's up to you if these kinds of anthro birds or bats can still fly or not in your own world. Perhaps your birds or bats have lost flight. For bird species, if they can't fly, do they still have feathers on their arms or not?

A third option is to keep the species' wings and not give them hands at all. Like the hooves above, if you go this route keep in mind this will affect your world-building. Your winged species might have trouble manipulating things without hands, having to rely on their feet, beak, or mouth. This will be covered later in the world-building and character sections. An example of this option can be seen in the bat character from *Sixes Wild* by Tempe O'Kun.

Claws

If the species you are anthropomorphizing has claws, you'll need to decide if they keep them or not in their anthro form. Do cats still have retractable claws? Do those claws ever snag on their clothes?

Do birds still have talons for feet? Does this affect their ability or desire to wear shoes?

These decisions will affect your world-building.

Horns/Antlers

Like claws, if your species had horns or antlers, decide if the anthro version still has them. They don't have to! Or they could have less pronounced versions. However, it can add a fun aspect to your world-building to force antlered characters to wrestle with the problems inherent to having large, awkward, poky structures atop their heads. What does this mean for clothing and architecture in their world? Are some doors simply too small? Can the antlered animals wear pull-over sweaters?

Tails

Anthro characters are usually written to still have tails, although removing them is also a valid option, as in the *Night in the Woods* video game.

Be aware that even if your text explicitly says your species doesn't have tails that fans might still add them in fan art or fan fiction. Many furry readers are big fans of tails and so you remove them at your peril.

However, tails also are a big world-building sticking point. You'll have to consider them in architecture, furniture, clothing, body language, and more. Though doing so is often much of the fun in writing furry fiction.

Fangs and Beaks

Does the anthro version of your species still have a beak or fangs? If so, does this affect their ability to smile or otherwise communicate with standard human facial expressions? However, even if your character's face isn't built for smiling, you can do a lot of non-verbal communication through head tilts, crinkles around the eyes, or movement of the ears.

Diet and Teeth

What does your anthro eat? Is it the same as the wild version, or do they now eat a human diet? Can dogs eat chocolate, or will it poison them like in real life? If you don't deal with this question explicitly, you'll likely have readers who own dogs cringing inwardly and worrying for any dog characters whenever they eat chocolate. It's better to explicitly state that the chocolate won't hurt them.

If you have both anthro or intelligent carnivores and herbivores in your world, this will give you some fun world-building options later, as you try to address the question of how carnivores get their meat, and how that affects their relationship with any herbivores in the world.

- Carnivores - meat eaters. Obligate carnivores eat solely meat or animal tissue (example, tigers) while facultative carnivores will also sometimes consume other things (example, bears). They have almost entirely sharp teeth.
- Omnivores - consume both meat and plants. Combination of wide flat teeth in the back and sharper teeth in the front for tearing.
- Herbivores - consume plant matter. Will have wide flat teeth.

Active Time Period

What times of day is your anthro species usually awake and when do they sleep? Of course, this will vary by individual, but you're deciding right now on the average of this anthro species.

Options:
- Diurnal - most active during the day and sleep at night.
- Nocturnal - most active during the night and sleep during the day.
- Crepuscular - most active during twilight. Some crepuscular species are also active in bright moonlight and overcast days.
- Cathemerality - active period shifts from diurnal to nocturnal depending on the time of the year.

This can always change from individual character to character of the same species. Perhaps your bat character enjoys being out during the day. However, if by and large, bat society happens at night, they may have trouble making friends, be sleepy while trying to do tasks that require them to be up at night, or run into other issues stemming from their backwards sleep schedule.

Size

How tall are your anthros? If your starting species is very small, like a mouse or a Chihuahua dog, is the anthro version of your species still small? Be aware that it might throw some readers out of immersion if you have mice that are taller/larger than tigers. Though, the rules may be different if you've chosen for your furry characters to be of the gene-modded human type, since then they'd all be starting out as vaguely human-sized before being altered.

Coloring

What color fur/skin/scales does your anthro species have? Do they have a more natural range of colors like their wild counterparts? Do they have stripes or spots?

Do male and female individuals tend to have different color patterns? For instance, calico cats in real life are predominantly female, since the genes for orange and black fur are both carried on the X chromosome, meaning that male cats generally only have one or the other of those colors. So, perhaps the rare male calico chooses to dye his fur to be more monochromatic, or else he embraces his unusual coloring, making it a quirky and interesting part of his personality.

Decide what is common. Of course, dye, tattooing, and other body modifications are possible, but here we're only focused on their 'natural' colors. Any shade can be 'natural' for your species, it's fiction after all!

For example, maybe your space foxes can have fur ranging from neon yellow to pink, but will never have blue fur (unless they dye it, of course). Conveying a sense of what's typical for your species will allow readers to recognize if a particular character doesn't follow the fold.

Habitat

Where can this animal commonly be found? Are they desert dwelling? Aquatic? Tropical?

In a story, your characters will commonly venture out of their comfort zones as part of the call to adventure, so you'll need to know what kind of habitat or temperatures they are used to. A tropical bat will probably struggle in northern Russia with the cold and the dry air, but a polar bear might feel right at home - even if they grew up in the tropics.

Use the internet or books to research if you have questions about a particular species. Think about what the baseline for your species is and what they might have to do to adapt to different regions of the world.

This applies as much to your squirrel visiting her starfish friend under the sea as it does to your polar bear going on a tropical vacation. The squirrel is obviously going to need a breathing apparatus of some type, but the polar bear might need accommodations as well, like a chilled room for when they get too hot.

If you have an alien species or an aquatic one, you'll have to address the question of what they breathe and whether or not they can be out of water for too long without drying out.

Secondary Sex Characteristics & Reproduction

Sexual dimorphism - if your starting species has markedly different sexual characteristics, does your anthro species share that difference? What sets the females of your species apart from the males, visually, at a glance. It may be nothing, or they might look completely different, like male and female angler fish or peacocks.

Reproduction - do they still reproduce the same way? Do they have litters instead of, typically, one child at a time? How does this affect sibling dynamics and family size?

Do egg-layers still lay eggs to reproduce in their anthro form? What about those species that abandon their young, such as the giant Pacific octopus which can lay 20,000 - 100,000 eggs at a time? There are fascinating world-building options for dealing with these sorts of traits, but they can also lead you down rabbit holes that will take you off track from the story you want to write. It's okay to discard natural animal traits when designing your anthro version if that's what works best for you.

Human-like genitalia - Does your species have the same genitalia as their wild counterparts, or are they more human? (This might only matter if you plan to have an erotica scene. Feel free to skip this if you feel it doesn't apply to your work.)

Leading into... (Yes, you knew this was coming)

Breasts - does your anthro species have human-like breasts? (Yes, human titties on, for example, a snake, is a bit silly. But it's your writing! Go forth and write it if you want!) This question also relates back to the matter of reproduction - if your species typically reproduces in litters and breastfeeds, then they may be endowed with more than two breasts.

Other Characteristics

Be sure to consider other possible physical traits that your species might have. A few examples might be:

Fish/octopus/shark anthros - can they still breathe underwater? Can your whale anthros still swim deep in the ocean?

Skunk/ferret anthros - do they still have their scent glands that allow them to spray/stink?

Can your octopuses still spray ink?

Do your deep-sea creatures have the ability to communicate using sound, or do they communicate using color patterns on their skin?

Snake/scorpions, other things with venomous bites - are they still venomous or poisonous?

Do your lizards or dragons shed their skins?

This also would include any other characteristics you'd like to give your species. Do they have magical powers? Can they walk on water? Mind-reading? The possibilities are endless!

You'll want to, at least, have the basic rules of your world nailed down before you begin writing. It's no fun to have to rewrite huge sections of text because you did not decide on the rules of your world before beginning to write. Spend a little bit of time now, to save lots of time in the future.

3.3. Furry Species Checklist - Feral

Due to the nature of a feral type species, this list will be shorter, but no less important. If you are building a feral species from scratch (perhaps you want a made-up chimera beast or an alien feral that doesn't have an Earth analogue), use the longer anthro checklist, mentally replacing anywhere it says 'anthro' with 'feral.' Otherwise, it is assumed here that your feral species will have the same characteristics as their Earth analogue.

Thumbs/Hand-like Paws

Is your feral limited to its real-world ability to manipulate objects with its paws/fins/wings/flippers/claws etc? Or does it have something like a thumb on its forepaws that allows it to manipulate things?

Does it have mental projection (telekinesis, ability to manipulate things with its mind) that allows it to simulate having hands? (For example, the unicorn's magic in *My Little Pony: Friendship is Magic* allows them to move objects around without actually touching them.)

Talking

Can your feral speak to the other species in your world out loud?

This can change from species to species. Maybe you are doing a Secret World of Animals story, so your feral dogs can speak to other dogs, cats, rabbits, mice, and other animals, but not to the humans in the story.

Even if your species can speak out loud, are they speaking the same language?

Can they hear each other (maybe one speaks in too high a pitch to even be heard by some other species)? Maybe they can only speak underwater, use some variety of sign language, or depend on color-changing skin (like octopuses) to communicate using a visual language.

Size

How big are your animal characters? You'll need two measurements - snout to tail and feet to back. These don't need to be exact, but you'll want to know if your feral comes up to your human or anthro's knees or hips and how tall they might be if they stand on their hind legs. Maybe later they need to bite the bad guy's face or take something off a tall table. Could they do it easily or would they need to manipulate something to climb or jump?

Even if you don't precisely describe the size of your character, readers will be looking for clues as to their size, so it's important to have their size clear in your head while writing.

Coloring

The questions to consider here are mostly the same as with anthro characters. Knowing what's typical for your species will help you know how to refer to them as you write.

However, one aspect to consider that's unique to feral type characters with respect to coloring is: can you tell the talking versions of the animals apart from normal, non-talking counterparts by special color patterns? Perhaps talking skunks always have a triple-striped tail, and so they're able to recognize each other before speaking.

Secondary Sex Characteristics & Reproduction

Generally feral style furry characters stay more similar to their real-world analogues than anthro style characters do, so you likely have fewer choices to make with regards to secondary sex characteristics and reproduction here. However, it's still worth keeping these traits in mind and making conscious choices about whether you want to alter your furry species from how they work in the real world or not.

3.4. Other Things to Keep in Mind

Remember as you build your species, think about what works best for the story *you* have in mind. Don't make a decision because "it's always done that way." Make sure it is the best decision for your story. You are the ultimate judge, jury, and executioner... no wait, that's a bad metaphor.

Let's start over. There are no *correct* answers to the questions above. None. You are the Ultimate God-Architect of your world. The Story Master. What you say, goes.

If you make a choice, and later it's not working or you suddenly don't like it? Change it! Your answers here are not carved in stone.

For example, if you make an anthro swan species with wings and arms, and in the middle of writing you realize it's too much work trying to figure out what to do with their wings when they are not flying, go ahead and change it so that they have wing arms with hands at the end. Mark the place in your manuscript where you made the change so you know you'll need to revise previous sections in your second draft and update your world dictionary.

Earlier we mentioned you can save a lot of time by nailing these issues down ahead of time, but you make the best decision you can at the time. There's no harm in changing it mid-text, other than the time you'll need to spend revising the earlier portion of your manuscript or story.

It can even be possible to retroactively alter your world-building after a piece is published. In Mary's *Otters in Space* series, the first book establishes that octopus women generally die after laying their eggs, like in real life. By book 3, Mary regretted this choice and revealed that the character who had shared this information had been raised in a traditionalist cult, and actually, most women octopuses no longer died after laying their eggs.

World-building should be fun. Don't let yourself get trapped into a world you aren't happy with. When it's your world, you have the power to change it.

Part 4: World-building

4.1. Species Affects Setting

When building your world, be sure to keep your species in mind. Even in a modern-day contemporary setting, you'll need to think through how things might be different if things were built by an anthro species. For instance, the houses designed for otters in Kyell Gold's *Waterways* have swimming pools instead of normal floors and the space stations in Mary's *Otters in Space* have rivers running through them.

4.2. World Dictionary

A World Dictionary is a document that you use to keep track of the details of your world, such as your species details; your characters, from their names, species, occupations, likes, dislikes, quirks; and your setting.

This document can be anything - a text file, a paper notebook, a personal wiki, a pile of post it notes, or a specialized program like World Creator, World Anvil, or Plottr.

Be sure not to overdo it at this step. It's easy to get lost in world-building and never make it to actually writing a story.

You'll need to know your main and supporting characters and species, and a few details of the setting before you start writing, but you don't need detailed maps of everything in your entire world before you start. You can keep adding to, and developing, your world-building as you go along. And remember, the real world keeps changing; it's possible for fictional worlds to change as your story develops too.

4.3. Settings

Setting can be both macro and micro in scope. A macro example of setting would be the question: is this set on modern-day Earth or a secondary world? A secondary world can be anything from a magical land with mages and dragons that's entirely your own, to a different planet, possibly in the same universe as modern-day Earth.

A micro example of setting would be building out the places important to the story. For example, you'll need to be able to picture the house your main character lives in, and the city that house resides in, when you're describing your character moving through their day.

It's important that the macro and minor settings work together as a cohesive whole. If your macro setting is a distant alien planet, it probably won't make sense if your characters live in modern-day New York City. But perhaps a group of former New Yorkers traveled to this distant planet and founded a city? Your characters could live in New York Settlement, perhaps famous for the fondness for pizza and tall buildings brought along by the original founders.

Be sure to take into account your species when creating your setting. A city built by anthro beavers will probably look much different than one founded by anthro seagulls. While both would probably settle on the water, a beaver city would probably be mostly or partially underwater, with wood or mud-daub houses and swimming channels. A seagull city would be all above water with lots of perches and docks to fish off of with the housing being high up in trees or on stilts.

Think about the history of a place as well. Is your city brand new, with plenty of space to expand and newly built houses or is it an old city that might be running out of room and feature lots of run-down or historical housing mixed with more modern construction?

These are the kind of details that can be thrown into a text with just a line or two, providing a layer of detail that adds a lot of depth to a story and draws readers into the world, making it feel real to them.

For example, in Ian's Sam Digger stories, the animal anthros have rebuilt on the ruins of old human structures. A family of Texas Longhorn cattle have taken over an old human ranch house, widening the doors to fit their massive horns, and building on more barn-like expansions to the original house.

In Mary's *Otters in Space*, the cats and dogs live in a world where the humans have disappeared. Repurposed old human buildings have massive doors and vaulted ceilings from the point of view of the much smaller cats and dogs. Newly built structures are made at a smaller scale more suited to their shorter height.

In a secondary world example, in Ryan Campbell's *Koa and the Drowned Kingdom*, the bats and otters live in giant mangrove trees, with the otters living around the roots near the water and the bats living up on the higher levels of the tree in the branches.

4.4. Culture

Think about the kinds of things your races might celebrate. Festivals or holidays can be tied to a religion, a season, or a phase of life.

What might your races worship? What is their religion? Really dig into your species and think about what might make sense for them.

What would they celebrate?

Perhaps a bird race that eats bugs might celebrate the start of spring, when all the insects start re-emerging or hatching, with a grand feast or festival celebration.

An alligator race that hibernates in winter might have one last hurrah before everyone goes to ground for the cold season, a chance to say goodbye.

In Mary's *Entanglement Bound*, there is a race of butterfly aliens that have a Wing Day coming-of-age celebration for when their young emerge from their chrysalises after changing from their child larva form to a young adult form with wings which are then ceremonially cut off, since they're vestigial.

In a similar vein, in Ian's *Flower's Fang* novel, the plant-like Kin have a celebration when their young pull out of the dirt for the first time.

Religion and culture is a great place to build out conflict in your world as well. Think about how many wars have started over culture clashes or religion in the real world.

Your bat species might venerate the moon and the stars while your birds worship the sun.

Just remember, this is at a species level. Your actual characters might not be religious at all or partake in a religion that's unusual for their species. This might even be a source of tension between your character and the greater whole of their species if they are an outlier.

Perhaps one of your bats married a bird and converted to sun worship. Holidays at home might be a little tense during the moon ceremonies if that bat now refuses to participate.

In Mary's world of *Otters in Space*, the dogs worship the missing humans, "The First Race," and preach that they are just protecting things until the humans return. Most cats are not believers in the Church of the First Race, and the occasional one who is, is seen as strange by the other cats. Not every dog is a believer either.

4.5. Language

While obviously your books will be written in whatever human language you speak, you can add some color and depth to your world by considering how language might change for whatever species you are writing about.

Consider carefully your species and how that might change the way they communicate.

Bee characters might dance to speak, while a bird would sing, a cricket rub its legs together to talk via humming, or an octopus and cuttlefish might use changing body color to communicate.

A great example is in S. Park's short story "Colored in Sepia" that features cuttlefish talking both with body color and words. Also, the octopuses in Mary's *Otters in Space* series communicate emotion with their skin color and more complex language using their tentacles to speak in a sign language that has to be adapted for otters who don't have the advantage of eight tentacles for signing but also need to communicate underwater.

Mira Grant's mermaids in *Into the Drowning Deep* also use sign language to communicate.

Think about body language as well. Your dog characters' tails and ears can say a lot about their feelings, in a way that a human character can't replicate. A dog might have a hard time reading excitement from humans, with their lack of tails.

A dragon or lizard with their lack of facial expressions might not understand a cat's pulled back lips meaning that it's angry.

A great example of unique species language in fiction can be seen in Phillip Pullman's *The Amber Spyglass*. A human woman ends up in a land populated by sentient elephant-like creatures called Mulefa that communicate by making gestures with their trunks. Eventually the human woman figures out how to mimic their speech by using her arms wrapped together so that they can talk.

Along with this, think about swearing. Every species will have some way of insulting another, and that might change vastly between species and can be a great source of conflict and tension in your writing. For example, perhaps you have a character that is a cat. She might greatly offend a bird character by flicking her tail in irritation, which to that bird species is a grave insult.

4.6. Clothing

What are your characters wearing? It might be nothing! Maybe your anthro cats consider fur enough and only bother wearing clothing when doing dangerous work that requires PPE (personal protective equipment). Or maybe they only dress up for parties and special occasions.

A duck character, for instance, who uses its arm-wings for flight might not want anything constricting its upper body, so only wears pants.

Tails and wings both greatly affect clothing choices, same with taur species. Maybe for tailed characters their pants snap closed in the back as well as the front, in order to accommodate different sized tails across species in ready-to-wear mass-produced clothing.

Taur species, with their more feral-like bodies might only wear tops and draping coverings over their backs.

An otter might prefer wet-suits or quick-dry clothing if they are going to be getting in and out of the water frequently.

In Gre7g Luterman's *Kanti Cycle* books, the main species, the geroo, are a kangaroo-like species who do not wear clothing. They do like jewelry and accessories, as well as arm-band pouches that they use to carry things.

Gre7g Luterman has also married religion with the geroo's clothing. Part of the accessories the geroo wear is an ancestor necklace that they only take off in death or when exchanging beads with a lover. Geroo who have exchanged necklace beads are considered married. Dead geroo's beads are displayed in a family shrine in a corner of the house in a form of ancestor worship.

This is an excellent example of several levels of world-building through clothing; the geroo are able to wear so little because they live on spaceships and space stations that have constant temperatures and no atmospheric conditions like rain or snow that they have to worry about.

Think about the setting that you've chosen. What makes sense for the climate as well as the species?

A thick-furred leopard might not need more than a thin cotton shirt and pants in places with a mild winter, but your naked mole rat or tropical parrot might be bundled up in a thick coat and hat in the same weather. Conversely, if you set another scene of that same book during summer, your leopard might be far too hot no matter what they wear, while your mole-rat might have to be careful to protect their skin to prevent sunburn.

Clothing and accessories can also be used to denote your character's status. Are they poor or wealthy? A poor character may be wearing much different clothing than a rich character of the same species from the same location/setting.

Species might value different things. A crow character might be all about the shiny, no matter if it's a shimmering gem or a reflective piece of foil. Crow status might be denoted by the amount and type of shinies in or on their outfit. A rich crow might be decked out in gold and gems, where a poor crow might stitch reflective candy wrappers that they found in the garbage to their pants in an attempt to add some sparkle to their outfit.

Also think about gender when world-building your clothing. Some species have large degrees of sexual dimorphism where others might not. How do they use or not use clothing to display their gender? This part is entirely up to you.

Maybe you have a bird species with very large sexual dimorphism between the males and females, let's say peafowl. If you take it one direction, peacocks and peahens don't have a different dress code because it's so easy to tell them apart by color. OR maybe your peacocks dress up as gaily as their feathers and the peahens wear drab clothing to match theirs, or vise-versa and the peahens wear lots of color to offset their drab feathers while the males wear drab clothing to make their bright feathers stand out.

Each option says very different things about peafowl society in your world, so think about the story you are trying to tell!

Part 5: Characters

5.1. Choosing Species

The first question a lot of people ask is, "What species should I make my main character?" The answer is: whatever species best fits the story you want to write!

There are two main approaches you could take: decide the species first and then build out your character, basing their background and personality on the species OR decide on all the personality and background traits of your character and then pick a species to match or artfully contrast with those traits.

Fursonas

So, we're not going to come right out and say not to use your fursona, if you have one, as the character you're going to write about, but... maybe reconsider if you plan to eventually publish your written work or submit your stories to anthologies.

First of all, you probably feel very strongly about that character. They are deeply personal to you, but you need to be able to deal objectively with the characters in your fiction.

Secondly, you *are* going to get bad reviews. This is inevitable for any written work. (And if you don't believe us, go look up your absolutely favorite novel on your favorite review site, and click on the 1 or 2 star reviews.)

How are you going to feel when those negative reviews are about your fursona and their story? The reviews are likely to feel a lot more personal that way.

Our advice: if you really want to write about them, use the same species as your fursona but make a new character, perhaps similar in many ways, but still separate and distinct. This will make it easier to separate yourself from your character when receiving harsh reviews or even simple suggestions for changes from an editor.

Pick by Need

For some stories the species is determined by the call. A call is a posting inviting people to submit stories for publication to a particular market, and some markets will only consider stories about specific animals.

If the call requires a wolf character or a mythical like a dragon in order to be considered, the first thing you'd do is figure out which character that is going to be. Once that's done, then you can start fleshing out the rest of the cast around them.

When Ian wrote *Ritual of the Ancients*, he knew a character needed to be a jackal because of the link to Egyptian mythology that was woven into the rest of the story. In the mythology, jackals are guardians of the dead, and the main character is a vampire. So, he chose to make the love interest a jackal shifter.

Picking Something You Like

If you look at our stories, you'll see that Ian has written more than one featuring Chihuahuas, and a whole novel series with a dog-like race. Whereas, Mary's books and stories tend to center on a feline protagonist, often with dog or otter friends.

Don't be afraid to pick a particular species just because you like them. Writing comes from the heart, so if there's an animal close to your heart, you may find that writing about that species simply comes more easily and pulls the stories out of you.

Don't fight your instincts here. Let yourself write the stories that are in your heart. That's the reason writers get drawn to furry fiction in the first place - they'd rather tell stories about an animal that interests them than yet another story filled with humans like we see every day in the real world.

Picking a Species for its Uniqueness

Another option is to pick something unique. Maybe a platypus, just because you've never seen a story about one before and think it'd be fun. Go for it! That is a totally valid reason to pick a particular species, and it can immediately lead you to interesting questions that will help draw you through the process of creating your story — what's it like inside a platypus's head? What does a platypus want from life? How is a story made different and interesting by the main character being a platypus? Figure out your own answers to those questions, and you'll find yourself halfway through creating a story outline.

Pick a Species as a Foil to another

By foil here we mean two species that contrast with each other and possibly have a lot of potential for conflict with each other, simply due to what they are. If you've already created some of your cast, you can always flesh it out more by picking a species as a foil to another. Or start out picking two characters at once by using the foil method.

Some foils might be predator and prey (cheetah and a zebra), large and small (elephant and a mouse), water and land (octopus and a cat), scaled and furred (gecko and a raccoon), etc. The possibilities are nearly endless.

An example of a casting choice like this would be Judy, the rabbit, and Nick, the fox, from the movie *Zootopia*; Mary's Lashonda and Topher from *When a Cat Loves a Dog*; or Ian's beaver that goes on a blind date with a Texas Longhorn steer in "Blind Date Blues."

Picking at Random

If you're struggling with somewhere to start when picking a species, there are several options. One valid method, that both Mary and Ian use quite often, is to pick at random. This often works better for background characters than main characters, who usually have more constraints on them. But if it works for you, it's a completely valid way to go.

There are websites you can go to that will give you a random animal. There are links to a few in the Resources section at the end.

Drawing a random card from a deck of animal cards is another option. There are multiple animal card decks for sale online, or you can make your own with blank cardstock. We also include a Furry Story Roll-Up in the resources at the end of the book that will allow you to pick a random animal by rolling dice.

No matter your method, picking random animals for your characters can be fun and inspiring. If the first one you pick doesn't call to you, keep drawing until you find one that does. You can always make the other animals you drew into side characters. Sometimes, the combination of characters created by drawing random animals, that you never would have picked to put into a story together, can lead to exciting pieces of fiction. It can be fun to surprise yourself with your own writing by pushing outside your comfort zone, and writing new types of characters or even weird combinations of animals.

5.2. Species leads to Personality

Generally, it's common for furry writers to pick the species of a character before beginning to develop the personality of that character. This makes a lot of sense, as the species of a character will have a big effect on possible personalities for that character. Here are a couple of examples.

Random Example 1 - Gene-modded Fox

Let's start fleshing out a few hypothetical characters by starting with the species, just to show it can work.

Imagine an anthology call for stories about foxes. If you want to submit to this anthology, you'll need to write a story with a fox character. But which character?

First, you need to consider the story you want to write and go through Part 2 to figure out Type (in this case you already know Species) and if your fox will be feral or anthro. Let's say you decide to write a gene-modded human character who is an anthro fox. For this example, these choices were chosen at random. You can do the same, or else make choices based on what options call to you at the time.

In this example, if you want your fox character to be more sympathetic, you'll probably want to make them the protagonist or a character close to the protagonist. We'll pick the protagonist for this example.

Is the character fighting against the typical fox stereotypes or are they playing into them? Maybe the answer to this question plays into why the character might have decided on a fox-form gene modification, making them into an anthro fox in the first place.

In fact, that's a good place to start building out this character - why would this person decide on a fox out of all the possible animals? Maybe they just like foxes and didn't think about the stereotypes associated with them. If so, what is it that they like about foxes? Their grace? Their cunning? Their bright orange fur?

If the character chose to become a fox without thinking about the stereotypes associated with foxes, then we're likely dealing with an impulsive character who might make other choices without thinking them through.

Of course, once the character has done the modifications and becomes a fox, they'll start discovering that people make certain assumptions about who they are based on that choice. The next step for you, as the author, would be to figure out how the character feels about those assumptions. Are they bothered by the assumptions? How do they react? By answering these questions, you'll start learning more about the kind of person the character is, and you can begin exploring how that person will move through the world in your story.

Random Example 2 - Antelope Centaur

Perhaps you want to stretch your writing out of your comfort zone, so you decide to use a random animal generator and get a Pronghorn antelope; then on another random generator for type, you get mythical. A little goggling tells you that antelopes are prominent in Native American mythology, but you don't want to go that direction. So, you decide to make the character you're developing an antelope centaur.

So, you have a centaur. That immediately says fantasy, but centaurs in fantasy have been done a lot. What about a sci-fi centaur?

Perhaps you like the idea of a mechanical centaur who works on a spaceship. This character is probably adventurous, because she does deep space work that requires spacewalking. (Also, who isn't intrigued by the idea of a centaur in a space suit?) This choice is also interesting because it removes the main advantage that centaurs have - their four horse-like limbs that allow them to move very quickly on land.

What kind of advantages (or disadvantages) might the mecha-antelope-centaur have in space? Think about the obstacles this character would have had to face to even become a deep space mechanic. Perhaps she's had to overcome a lot of discrimination, but still managed to achieve her dream of space flight. Now that she's working in space, perhaps she finds that her extra limbs while wearing magnetic boots allow her to move more freely on the outer hull of the spaceship, making her invaluable when it comes to outside repairs.

We'll stop here with this example, but this should give you an idea of how to start developing a character out of the choices you make, whether randomly or based on your own preferences.

There are lots of books about building out a character once you've gotten this far. We'll put some of our recommendations in Part 6.

Personality Leads to Species

Another way to build a character is to decide who they are - what their personality and quirks are like, or what role they'll play in the story - and then pick a species to match or artfully conflict with those choices.

For instance, when Mary set out to write *The Snake's Song*, she knew the main character would spend most of the novel in an underground labyrinth, feeling lost and out of their element, searching for hidden treasures, since the book was designed to be part of the *Labyrinth of Souls* series. Eventually, she settled on making the main character a squirrel - an animal that generally doesn't belong underground and who's known for seeking out buried stashes of treasure.

Part 6: Writing

6.1 Write a Story

At some point, you need to move on from just world-building and figuring out the details of your characters to actually writing a story about them, because that's where the real magic happens. When the words hit the page, you get to see your ideas metamorphose from amorphous concepts in your head into an actual story that you can share with the world.

There are some basic tenets for story-writing - figure out something that your character wants and doesn't have, then show how they try to get it; mix descriptive passages and dialogue together in a way that keeps the plot moving and readers engaged; and place your story at a point in the character's life when something is changing. But overall, the topic of how to write a story is far too large to cover in depth here.

How to write a story is a topic large enough to be an entire book all on its own, and the focus of this text is specifically on how to make your story and characters furry. Our assumption is that you already know the basics of how to start writing your story, but are just struggling to give it that fun, colorful, furry edge.

If you do need help with the mechanics of general story-writing, there are lots of great writing books out there, and we've listed some of our favorites below.

Damn Fine Story: Mastering the Tools of a Powerful Narrative by Chuck Wendig - This covers how to set up your storytelling to make your readers care about your characters. It covers visualizing storytelling, character relationships, rising and falling tension, and developing themes.

Create a Plot Clinic by Holly Lisle - This is the book to pick up if you don't even know where to begin starting your story. It includes lots of activities and exercises on how to brainstorm up plot points, characters, and settings, then goes over how to turn those into a cohesive whole. The exercises are also useful if you are stuck and don't know where to go next. This is the book Ian references most frequently.

How to Write a Novel Using the Snowflake Method by Randy Ingermanson - This is the book to start with if you have a base idea that you want to expand into a short story or a novel. It covers how to turn a small idea into a full narrative by adding a tiny detail at a time.

Take Off Your Pants! by Libbie Hawker - This book covers how to outline a traditional hero's journey story. The focus is on adding specific story beats, but it also covers pacing. A hero's journey focuses on one specific character who will complete a solitary quest.

The Heroine's Journey by Gail Carriger - This book covers the beats of a heroine's journey story using examples from myth and modern popular fiction. A heroine's journey is a story about a group of characters working together towards a common goal.

Romancing the Beat by Gwen Hayes - This book specifically talks about how to set up a traditional romance story, highlighting the story beats (emotional high and low points) that romance readers are looking for.

Wonderbook: The Illustrated Guide to Creating Imaginative Fiction by Jeff Vandermeer - This is the most eclectic book of the list. Each illustrated 2-page spread covers a topic of writing, outlining, or narrative fiction. It includes interviews with other authors about various writing topics. It's visually very interesting and great if you are more of a visual learner. Very fun to flip through, and each section by itself is a quick read, perfect for short attention spans.

2k to 10k: Writing Faster, Writing Better, and Writing More of What You Love by Rachel Aaron - "Why are you including this book about writing faster?" - we already hear you asking. Because this book covers some great points about outlining that are very important and hinted at in the title. It teaches you how to write more of what you love and about how to outline a story that you and your readers will love.

6.2. Make It Furry

Beyond basically knowing how to write fiction, Step 1, of course, in writing a furry story is to make sure you say what species your characters are in the text, whether explicitly or indirectly in a way the reader will understand.

Ian and Mary have each read plenty of stories in slush piles where they've gotten all the way to the end without being able to figure out what kind of animal the characters are. This is not good, and leaves your reader puzzling their way through the story, instead of relaxing and enjoying it.

For an alien species, what earth animal are they most like? It's perfectly fine to call them 'fox-like' or "a combination of an octopus and a dog." Those are reference points your readers will understand, and clarity is a valuable trait in any kind of writing, including fiction.

Of course, for more unusual or uncommon species you'll need to throw in a description as well. Although honestly, this is probably a good idea at some point even for a common species, since even two animals of the same species are not going to look identical, and furthermore, descriptions of animals are part of what draws readers to furry fiction.

Say you've made the two main species in your story anthro zebras and anthro okapis. Your readers probably know what a zebra looks like, but maybe not an okapi. In this case, one way you could gracefully inform them would be to highlight the similarities and differences between the more familiar and less familiar species.

You could mention that the zebra might not know what to make of the male okapi's ossicones (flesh covered horns), but be attracted to the okapi anyway because of the black and white stripes on his legs and his long thin tail with the puff of hair on the end that looks like a zebra's.

So, you've identified your characters' species and given at least a cursory description of them. But you're not done yet. You'll need to keep reminding your readers throughout the story.

Just because the characters in your head are vibrant and alive, and you could never imagine them being different species than they are... that's not true for the reader until you make it true. So, until the reader gets to really know your characters, you'll have to keep reminding them of who and *what* those characters are.

6.3 Use Vocabulary to Your Advantage

In furry fiction, the words 'hands' and 'feet' can be replaced with something more specific to the type of animal you're writing about, like paws or hooves. The only thing to be careful of here is that it can be confusing as to whether you mean hands or feet at some points when using a word like 'paws' that could refer to either or both. So, make sure that your meaning is either clear from context, or use a more specific term, like 'hand-paws,' 'hind-paws,' or 'foot-paws'; though words like these can quickly get old for the reader, so use them sparingly.

Some readers may have trouble picturing how a hoofed animal could have hands, so it might help to specify details such as "keratin tipped fingers," at some point, when referring to 'hoof-hands' or 'hoofed-hands."

It's also okay, once you've established what your character is, to simply use 'hands' and 'feet' when those are appropriate. Mix all these options up to best suit the flow and feel of individual sentences.

Or if you are writing an Anything Goes story, you might not even explain how a hooved character uses tools, and leave it up to the reader's imagination.

The verb 'to say' can be replaced with bark, woof, meow, cluck, hiss, neigh, bleat, howl, burble, or more. This both adds flavor to the text and can help remind the reader what type of species the character is, especially if there are many different species in your story.

Reference characters' tails, fur, expressive ears, or other distinctive features. Even better if they can use them in ways a human can't.

Have your dog character wag their tail. Your giraffe bump their head on the ceiling.

A mouse in a world of taller animals might struggle to reach door knobs. An elephant might not fit through doorways.

A great white shark nurse may fight his instincts not to bite a bleeding patient (which opens a whole other question about this character and why they chose the profession they did).

One cat character might lick the fur of their arm to calm down when stressed, but a second cat character might find that archaic habit disgusting and thrash the tip of their tail instead.

These are just examples, of course. By now you should know your characters and their species. Think of something quirky each of your characters could do that can remind the readers of their animal qualities, while at the same time showing a bit of their personality.

6.4. Researching

But, you say, I don't know what kind of quirks my animal might have! Or I don't know what they sound like! Or what they can do!

Well, you're in luck! This is the golden age for researching animals. It's usually good to start by looking up some background information on an animal, for which there are generally lots of articles available on the internet. If you want to go more in depth, check out a book on the species you're interested in. But, one of the most wonderful tools is the wealth of readily available animal videos these days.

Search online for videos about your animal, and you're almost certain to find a wealth of information. Documentaries, videos from people filming wild animals playing, or educational videos posted by zoos, aquariums, or wildlife safaris are all great places to get a chance to observe the animal you're studying almost as if you were actually there. Lots of zoos have live-stream cameras of various exhibits where you can watch the animals in real time.

Watch and pay attention to the way the animal moves when running and walking. How do they hold their tails? Their heads? What kind of rhythm do they have to their gait?

Look at them sleeping, eating, playing, and courting. Take notes about how you'd describe each movement. Look at their body language and think about how they're using their bodies to communicate with each other. How might those behaviors continue or be adapted if the animal is anthropomorphized?

Practice writing down descriptions of what you are observing. Keep a list of these observations handy as you write, to refer to as you are going.

Dogs tend to tuck their tails between their legs when anxious or scared, and lift it higher when excited or interested. While a happy cat walks with their tail held straight up at a ninety degree angle, a super scared cat will do the same but have the fur of their tail all puffed out.

These are behaviors that cats and dogs will be familiar with in themselves and others once they're anthropomorphized, and they'll either use them purposely to communicate or might try to hide them, as instinctual, but vestigial, remnants of their animal nature. Both options are rich for story-telling and characterization. We learn so much about furry characters by how they lean into or away from their basic animal natures.

Even mythical animals have real-life analogs (horses for unicorns, lizards or dinos for dragons, etc). For something like a Sphinx or a chimera, look at the parts making up your creature.

Of course, you don't have to use any of this, but it's a great place to start thinking about how to describe your fictional creatures on the page, to breathe life into them, and set them apart from humans. It might even give you new ideas for scenes or places you could take your plot.

Maybe your bird hides his face in his wing when embarrassed, and so misses seeing that the horse that just walked past him stole his purse.

6.5. What's the Twist?

Before you start plotting or writing, take time to think about why you want to have anthropomorphic characters in your story. What about the plot or story changes because you have anthropomorphic characters?

This can be something as small as your dog detective character using his nose to track down a suspect, or your otter character having a house with a pool that takes up most of the inside, like in Kyell Gold's *Waterways*.

If you can replace your character with a human without changing anything about the story, stop and re-evaluate. For some stories this might matter less, like in a Fox in Starbucks or Anything Goes setting. However, your reader should be able to remember your characters are not human, and it should improve your story for it to be furry, even if it's only because animals are fun to think about. This is where language comes in handy.

If you've taken your character into account while considering your plot, some of this should come naturally as you tell the story. Steer your outline to put your characters into situations that let their furry features shine.

When Ian was writing "Blind Date Blues," he knew that at some point he wanted the main character's beaver characteristics to save the day. Naturally, this led to the beaver's steer date, a species generally not known for their swimming prowess, falling into the river.

Think about what changes you could make to the plot that would allow you to highlight your character's uniqueness. Do you have a scene set at a research station? If you have a bird, put that station at the top of a cliff and have the cable car lines snap. Now they have to fly!

A bunch of nails have been strewn across the road. Your horse character doesn't mind being the one to sweep them up, because he has hooves that are impervious to the sharp nails.

Of course, it doesn't have to be that dramatic, but you get the idea. Have your story do part of the work for you.

This example doesn't come from a novel, but it's a great one: at the end of *Kung Fu Panda*, it is a panda's strengths and the protagonist's very panda-nature that make him the perfect person to defeat the villain martial artist. When the furry nature of your characters comes back to play in unexpected, but natural-feeling ways like that, it can be very satisfying for the reader.

6.6. Sex Scenes (Optional)

As with any other furry fiction, if your story has scenes of a more intimate nature, ask yourself with them: what is the twist? What can you highlight about the characters during their intimate moments to remind the reader that they aren't human?

It can be as simple as a cat using their tail to stroke their lover in unusual places, or highlighting rough fur rubbing against another's back.

Animals might have different erogenous zones. In Francine DeCarey's *Dr. Bactrian and the Cursed Collar*, the camel protagonist's erotic zone is between her camel humps.

Get creative with it. In Tempe O'Kun's *Sixes Wild: Manifest Destiny*, the bunny character occasionally goes into heat, which causes her to take risks to reach her boyfriend that get her into trouble, and move the story along, and her boyfriend being a bat who often hangs upside down adds a whole other level.

In Ian's story "Milk and Brass," his swan character uses her feathers to tickle and tease her cat girlfriend, and in "The Literary Roleplay Club," his okapi character uses his long, flexible tongue to unique and powerful effect.

Try to have fun with it, as with all furry fiction, and work in the animal aspect.

6.7. Preventing Zipperbacks

A zipperback is a term for an anthro character who might as well be human, i.e. unzip the zipper at the back of their animal costume and you'll find a human. This term is usually said in a rude or condescending manner or used as an insult. It's generally applied to books where the characters do not use their animal characteristics during the story, to the point where you might even forget the characters aren't human as you are reading.

If you followed the advice in the rest of this book about clarifying and using your animals' characteristics and using words to highlight species, you shouldn't have a zipperback problem in your story.

However, if you do get that feedback, go back through the species checklist and try to mention each characteristic of your animal at least once. In a novel, try to hit each multiple times. For instance, if they have claws, mention the claws clicking when they pick up something hard or catching on their clothing. Remind the reader that these are animals.

Re-evaluate your usage of language to see if there are different words you can use to highlight your character's animal nature. Bleating is much more descriptive than said, as well as reminding readers that this character isn't human, and is, in fact, a goat.

Even small details can help cement the fact in your reader's minds and also help bring a story to life.

Review your story and see if there are any scenes that can be changed to highlight a feature of your main character's species. Either something that hinders them, like putting your bird underground, or helps them, like putting your bird in a situation where flying can save the day, or even just used to travel through the locations in your story.

6.8. Allegory

Furry fiction naturally lends itself to being seen through an allegorical lens. Sometimes this is intended by the author. For instance, George Orwell's *Animal Farm* is clearly meant as a political allegory, and *The Chronicles of Narnia* were intended by C.S. Lewis to be a religious allegory, even if many readers would prefer to overlook that aspect of the fun portal fantasies.

However, oftentimes readers will find allegory in furry fiction even when the author had no intention of their characters being taken as stand-ins for real world peoples or concepts. Partly, this may be because readers are trained to look for allegory in furry fiction by famous works like the aforementioned, but it's also just really easy to see groups of animals and imagine parallels between them and groups of people. So, as a furry writer, it's vitally important to stay aware of how your fiction might be interpreted if seen through an allegorical lens.

While it's absolutely possible to write simple, straightforward, fun to read stories about furry characters, it's also possible to find yourself saying things at an allegorical level that you wouldn't be comfortable with if confronted with them directly. And while you don't want to spend your time chasing after shadows, imagining every possible way that each and every sentence could be misinterpreted, you also don't want to make racist, queer-phobic, or generally bigoted statements, without realizing you're doing so, that cause your work to be received or age poorly.

For example, Brian Jacques' *Redwall* series is widely beloved among many furries, but it's also problematic and can make a lot of readers uncomfortable when seen allegorically. Throughout the series, prey animals like mice, moles, and hares are heroes, and predator species like weasels and foxes are the villains. At some level, this makes sense. If you create a furry world where some of the animals eat others, then the predators are going to be villains to the prey. However, the animals in the *Redwall* books generally don't eat each other, and occasionally, a character from a stereotypically evil species will attempt to become "good," only to be thwarted by their inherent nature. This naturally translates into the idea that some types of people are simply born bad and nothing they do will overcome it.

In the real world with humans, this idea translates to racism.

If that's not a message you want to send with your fiction (and it's not a message you should want to send), then you need to think about which animal species play what roles in your world, how changeable those roles are allowed to be, and how you handle that with your prose.

One of the most powerful works of furry fiction, *Maus* by Art Spiegelman, purposely uses animal species as stand-ins for different ethnicities and nationalities — mice are Jewish; cats are Nazis; pigs are Polish; and dogs are American. However, even though the allegorical use of animal species is purposeful, Spiegelman still takes time in his story to discuss the limitations of that representation. At one point, a character is depicted as both a mouse and a cat, because the narrator doesn't know if the imprisoned man was lying about his heritage. At another point, there's a discussion between the narrator and his wife — both mice — about how she should be depicted, since she converted to Judaism as an adult.

Discussing these kinds of edge cases — showing that there's fluidity between different categories and that none of your species consistently hold up as a clear allegorical stand-in for a specific group of people — can help keep unintended parallels from creeping into and gaining root in your stories.

Even so, it won't always be possible to stop readers from seeing parallels and reading into them. For instance, if a cat and an owl can fall in love in your world (which arguably, they can in the real world if you consider the real-life friendship between Fum & Gebra, and which they definitely do in the famous poem "The Owl and the Pussy-Cat" by Edward Lear), then a reasonable follow-up question is: can they also have biological children together? In the show *BoJack Horseman*, they likely could, and the resulting child would either be an owl or a cat. In the *Redwall* books, however, they couldn't. If they can't, then their relationship could be seen as metaphorical for relationships between humans who can't have biological children, and it's worth being sensitive to how it'll be seen when viewed in that light.

This doesn't mean that you have to write a world where owls and cats can procreate, but it does mean that if you're writing about an owl and cat who've fallen in love and want children, referring to their love as an abomination, a crime against nature, and profoundly wrong because of their inability to procreate could be read as betraying a bias against gay relationships or as an indictment of infertile couples. If that's not something you want to do (and again, we hope it's not something you want to do), then a little sensitivity while crafting your prose can go a long way.

With any fiction writing, it's worth keeping your own moral convictions in mind while crafting your stories. This goes doubly so for furry fiction. Readers will see race, gender, orientation, and every category that humans have ever been broken into reflected in furry characters. That's part of their power.

In conclusion, furry fiction is extremely charming and wonderful. The world needs more of it. Go forth and write!

Part 7: Appendix

7.1. Dictionary

Common Furry Species Terms:

- Avian - Broad term for birds
- Bovine - Broad term for cattle or cows
- Canine - Broad term for dogs, includes wild and domestic
- Cervidae - Broad term for deer or stags
- Equine - Broad term for horses
- Feline - Broad term for cats, includes wild and domestic
- Lapine – Broad term for rabbits
- Mammals - often used in place of human or people in a setting with no anthro birds or lizards
- Scalies or scaled - Broad term for lizards
- Taur - A species with a feral four-legged lower body and an anthro upper body
- Ungulate - Broader term for hooved animals like horses, zebras, rhinos, etc. Includes hooved and two-toed animals like pigs.

Active Period

- Diurnal - most active during the day and sleeps at night.
- Nocturnal - most active during the night and sleeps during the day.
- Crepuscular - most active during twilight. Some Crepuscular species are also active in bright moonlight and overcast days.
- Cathemerality - active period shifts from diurnal to nocturnal depending on the time of the year.

Diet

- Carnivores - meat eaters. Obligate carnivores eat solely meat or animal tissue (example, tigers) while facultative carnivores will also sometimes consume other things (example, bears). They have almost entirely sharp teeth.
- Omnivores - consume both meat and plants. Combination of wide flat teeth in the back and sharper teeth in the front for tearing.
- Herbivores - consume plant matter. Will have wide flat teeth.

7.2. Resources

Random Animal Generator Websites

https://www.generatorslist.com/random/animals/random-animal-generator - this one has a huge range of species and you can filter by general category (mammals, amphibian, bird, Reptile, etc) plus it gives you pictures of the resulting animals.

https://www.rangen.co.uk/world/speciesgen.php - Species generator, lets you mix and match form, type, size, and traits to let you get random hybrid creatures. Also has a bunch of other useful writing idea generators.

https://www.fantasynamegenerators.com/dragon-descriptions.php - Random dragon description generators. Site also has tons of other useful random generators for aliens, names, and more.

Furry Book Review Sites

Furry Book Review - written reviews of anthropomorphic literature. Runs the LEO Awards.

Dogpatch Press - Furry journalism blog that sometimes has guest book reviews

Claw & Quill - no longer active but has an archive of reviews of older works

Foalanblog - no longer active but has an archive of reviews of older works

Furry Writing Websites

Ursa Major Awards - https://ursamajorawards.org/

The Furry Writers' Guild - https://furrywritersguild.com/

The Cóyotl Awards - https://coyotlawards.com

Regional Anthropomorphic Writers Retreat -
http://www.rawr.community/

Leo Literary Awards–
https://furrybookreview.wixsite.com/blog/leo-awards

Downloadable Resources

Printable PDF versions of the following sheets can be
downloaded from https://madisonkeller.net/downloads/

Furry Story Roll-Up — Simple

Use this sheet, a six-sided die, and a twenty-sided die (or a number generator) to generate an inspirational starting point for writing a furry story!

Roll the six-sided die to choose a style of anthropomorphism:

1.Secret Life of Animals	4. Mythical Creatures
2.Uplifted by Science/Magic	5. Fox in Starbucks
3. Parallel Evolution/Aliens	6. Anything Goes

Roll the six-sided die to choose a secondary genre for your story:

1. High Fantasy	4. Romance
2. Mystery/Detective	5. Science-Fiction
3. Modern fantasy	6. Horror

Roll the twenty-sided die to pick the species of your primary character (roll twice for a hybrid):

1. cat	6.mouse	11.penguin	16.bear
2. otter	7.songbird	12.leopard	17.lion
3. eagle	8.fox	13.squirrel	18.rat
4. wolf	9.ferret	14.weasel	19.rabbit
5.dog	10.tiger	15.elephant	20.ostrich

Roll the twenty-sided die to pick the species of a secondary character (roll twice for a hybrid):

1.beaver	6.Lobster	11.deer	16.frog
2.bumblebee	7.walrus	12.antelope	17.tree
3.spider	8.sea lion	13.lizard	18.flower
4.guinea pig	9.horse	14.snake	19.chimpanzee
5.Dolphin	10.moose	15.sheep	20.giraffe

Roll the six-sided die to pick a relationship between these characters:

1. in love	3. mentor/acolyte	5. just met
2. abject hatred	4. family	6. work together

Roll the twenty-sided die to choose a setting (these could be on a distant planet or in a fantasy world):

1. school	6. car	11. playground	16. beach
2. hospital	7. sewers	12. train	17. police station
3. cafe	8. zoo	13. forest	18. jail
4. museum	9. laboratory	14. desert	19. fancy restaurant
5. wilderness	10. home	15. lake house	20. grocery store

Roll the twenty-sided die to choose a plot element or two:

1. time is running out	6. battling a nemesis	11. discovering a new culture	16. haunted by the past
2. questing for a valuable object	7. mistaken identities	12. time travel	17. hostage situation
3. keeping a secret	8. putting together a team	13. working for the enemy	18. thrust into leadership
4. lost	9. training for the championship	14. self-sacrifice	19. battle of wits
5. under pursuit	10. breaking into a fortress	15. learning a new skill	20. switching sides

Take these plot elements and characters and try to construct a story using them. If you need more characters or plot elements, feel free to roll-up some more. If you don't like something you've rolled, you can simply roll again. However writing a story with elements you wouldn't have chosen for yourself can lead to surprising and exciting twists!

Furry Story Roll-Up — Expanded

Use this sheet and a twenty-sided die (or a random number generator) to generate an inspirational starting point for writing a furry story!

Roll the die to choose a genre flavor (or two), since furry stories generally have secondary genres as well:

1. space opera	6. transformation	11. epic journey	16. detective
2. near future with uplift	7. mythical creatures	12. day in the life	17. crime
3. urban fantasy	8. mystery	13. medical drama	18. comedy
4. high fantasy	9. fairy tale	14. romance	19. heist
5. horror	10. buddy story	15. vignette	20. surrealism

Roll the die twice to pick a relationship between the characters at the beginning and end of the story - showing how they get from one state to the other will create an arc:

1. in love together	6. mentor/ acolyte	11. barely acquainted	16. manager and talent
2. abject hatred	7. family, or chosen family	12. work colleagues	17. total indifference
3. unrequited love	8. guide and follower	13. savior and distressed	18. each other's alibies
4. long lost friends	9. alternate timeline self	14. competitors	19. complete strangers
5. begrudging buddies	10. ghost and haunted	15. creator and creation	20. artist and muse

Roll the die to choose a setting (these could be on a distant planet or in a fantasy world):

1. school	6. car	11. playground	16. beach
2. hospital	7. sewers	12. train	17. police station
3. cafe	8. zoo	13. forest	18. jail
4. museum	9. laboratory	14. desert	19. fancy restaurant
5. wilderness	10. home	15. lake house	20. grocery store

Roll the die to choose a plot element or two:

1.time is running out	6.battling a nemesis	11.discovering a new culture	16.haunted by the past
2.questing for a valuable object	7.mistaken identities	12.time travel	17.hostage situation
3.keeping a secret	8.putting together a team	13.working for the enemy	18.thrust into leadership
4.lost	9.training for the championship	14.self-sacrifice	19.battle of wits
5.under pursuit	10.breaking into a fortress	15.learning a new skill	20.switching sides

Take these plot elements and characters (see the back) and try to construct a story using them. If you need more characters or plot elements, feel free to roll-up some more. If you don't like something you've rolled, you can simply roll again. However writing a story with elements you wouldn't have chosen for yourself can lead to surprising and exciting twists!

(See the next pages for a whole lot of animal grids!)

Roll the die to pick a grid (or choose one you like!), and then roll again to pick a species (repeat for a hybrid):

1-3:

1. cat	6. mouse	11. cheetah	16. bear
2. otter	7. guinea pig	12. leopard	17. lion
3. beaver	8. fox	13. squirrel	18. rat
4. wolf	9. ferret	14. weasel	19. rabbit
5. dog	10. tiger	15. elephant	20. sloth

4-6:

1. coyote	6. zebra	11. deer	16. goat
2. fennec fox	7. panda	12. antelope	17. kangaroo
3. hyena	8. koala	13. bison	18. gorilla
4. goose	9. horse	14. buffalo	19. chimpanzee
5. gazelle	10. moose	15. sheep	20. giraffe

7-9:

1. bluebird	6. emu	11. turkey	16. condor
2. ostrich	7. raven	12. vulture	17. chicken
3. penguin	8. crow	13. fruit bat	18. parrot
4. eagle	9.hummingbird	14. vampire bat	19. parakeet
5. hawk	10. nightingale	15. chickadee	20. lovebird

10-12:

1. walrus	6. hermit crab	11. electric eel	16. lantern fish
2. sea lion	7. octopus	12. whale	17. badger
3. dolphin	8. squid	13. shark	18. prairie dog
4. water skipper	9. fish	14. orca	19. meerkat
5. lobster	10. salmon	15. jellyfish	20. cuttlefish

13-15:

1.bumblebee	6.centipede	11. fire ant	16. locust
2. spider	7. praying mantis	12. moth	17.hornet
3. aphid	8. carpenter ant	13.grasshopper	18.wasp
4. butterfly	9.termite	14. firefly	19.tarantula
5.ladybug	10.cockroach	15.pill bug	20. earthworm

16-18:

1. lizard	6. turtle	11. hedgehog	16. clam
2. frog	7. tortoise	12. porcupine	17. reindeer
3. salamander	8. armadillo	13. pangolin	18. ocelot
4. gecko	9. anteater	14. capybara	19. possum
5. toad	10. platypus	15. mole	20. groundhog

19-20:

1. tree	6. velociraptor	11. pegasus	16. wyvern
2. flower	7. unicorn	12. cerberus	17. polar bear
3. fungus	8. brontosaurus	13. sea serpent	18. yak
4. dragon	9. jackalope	14. algae	19. alligator
5. tyrannosaurus	10. pterodactyl	15. chipmunk	20. crocodile

Furry Species Checklist - Feral

Species:

Ability to Manipulate items as if they had hands:

Yes / No / Limited

If yes or limited, write out the how and the limitations:

Ability to talk or communicate: Yes / No / Limited

If yes or limited, write out the how and the limitations:

Average Size:

Coloration - write out the natural colors and patterns:

Are all feral animals of this species intelligent? If not, is there a way to tell them apart visually?

Secondary Sex Characteristics:

Sex 1	Sex 2	Sex 3 or shared

Reproduction:

Life Cycle traits and length of time at each stage:

Baby	Teen	Adult	Old Age

Diet: Omnivore / Herbivore / Carnivore

Typical Diet

Active Period: Day / Night / Twilight / Shifting

Natural Habitat:

Body language (how does this species communicate through non-verbal cues):

Other Characteristics: (Wings / Horns / Venom / Poison / Spray / Etc)

Furry Species Checklist - Anthro

Species:

Origin Story / Type:

Hands – write terms used to refer to them and how they look/work:

Wings - Yes / No, write out the rules if yes:

Horns / Antlers - Yes / No, describe them if yes:

Tails - Yes / No, describe them if yes:

Average Height:

Coloration - write out the natural colors and patterns:

Secondary Sex Characteristics:

Sex 1	Sex 2	Sex 3 or shared

Reproduction – write out how it works:

Life Cycle, traits and length of time at each stage:

Baby	Teen	Adult	Old Age

Diet: Omnivore / Herbivore / Carnivore

Typical Diet

Active Period: Day / Night / Twilight / Shifting

Natural Habitat:

Body language (how does this species communicate through non-verbal cues):

Other Characteristics: (Venom / Poison / Spray / Etc)

Culture:

Holiday(s)/ Major Celebrations:

Major Religion(s) / Worship:

Typical Clothing:

About the Authors

IAN MADISON KELLER is a fantasy writer currently living in Oregon. Originally from Utah, he moved up to the Pacific Northwest on a whim a decade ago and never plans on leaving. Ian has been writing since 2013 with nine novels and more than a dozen published short stories out so far. Ian also wrote under the name Madison Keller before transitioning in 2019 to Ian. You can find him online at http://madisonkeller.net.

MARY E. LOWD is a prolific science-fiction and furry writer in Oregon. She's had nearly 200 stories and a dozen novels published, always with more on the way. Her work has won numerous awards, and she's been nominated for the Ursa Major Awards more than any other individual. Learn more at www.marylowd.com or read more stories at www.deepskyanchor.com.